this

is the

journey

alison malee

Also by Alison Malee

The Day Is Ready for You

Shifting Bone

this is the journey

alison malee

Andrews McMeel
PUBLISHING®

i have always collected words like paperweights.
little foreign objects. crisp clean feathers.
bulbs submerged and flourishing.
these ones, like the ones before, are for you.

for me, this book is a stillness. a sharing.
a telling and retelling. an awakening. a remembering.
a door. a lock. a key.

for you, this book can be anything.

the words can leave little imprints on your bones,

or hide away until you need them.

can build smoldering fires behind your eyes
or kiss you to sleep.

can haunt you or leave you no better and no
worse than before you read them.

my hope is that it may serve as a window.

a heart in hand. a quiet escape.

a fingerprint on the glass. a beckoning into the open.

the inhale before fresh air billows past the heartache.

a steadying breath.

contents

in the last ten years, i have lived in two countries,
three states, five apartments, and seven houses.
i learned how to drive, registered to vote,
became a college student.
i fell in and out of dangerous relationships,
rowed on a crew team,
discovered caffeinated chocolate bars,
and dropped out of college.

i moved to New York, drank too much alcohol,
and struggled to keep up with the rent.

i worked sixty-hour weeks at a karaoke bar.
i decorated doughnuts at a shop in Chelsea.
i took acting classes, auditioned for movies
and commercials.
i wrote stories on greasy napkins. i taught poetry
at a correctional center.
i met the love of my life.

in the last ten years, i have dyed my hair,
acquired four tattoos, and grown half an inch.

i have tracked down my biological family
and grown closer to my adopted parents.

i have gotten married, given birth to two miracles,
written three books, battled depression and anxiety,
and most importantly, grown into myself.

this book is the journey of my life
from adolescence to adulthood, from young woman
to mother.

it is a series of stories. a series of small,
intricate moments
i have collected, here, among these pages.
think of these words as a guide, as trial and error,
as permission to question everything.

i hope you know that this journey is messy.
it is murky. it is difficult.
it is not always going to be apparent that there is a
lesson in any of it.
lessons are usually tied to endings,
and the ending hasn't happened yet.

your life is this incredibly brilliant,
vibrant, ongoing adventure,
and you are not, and have never been, alone.

a beginning

this is a beginning.

a novel starts with
someone losing something beautiful or
finding something haunting.

a poem starts with someone sifting
through the remains of
what makes them human,

and then tumbling into the open like
scattered ashes.

like the wings of a great beast
encompassing everything.

a story takes shape first in the mind of
someone who understands
the world around them
to be a temporary place,

and then it unravels in the fingers.
in the pursuit of the right words.

a novel. a poem. a story.
a beginning.

it does not look like much,
but *this is mine.*

have we found it yet?

every road we travel
empties into alleys.
empties into trails.
empties into fields.
empties into valleys.

and, like light, we spill
from one home to the next.

not because
we want to leave
but because all we have
ever wanted is to find
somewhere
worth staying.

this is the journey

a woman yells at me on 14th street

sometimes the world watches us so closely,
i think they understand.
but even then, they miss all of the details of us.
the way our mouths stretch
from flat line to echoing laughter, slow and
    unapologetic.
the way joy shines through our teeth like everything
    is full.
how our cheeks flush when the steady rhythm
of the rain sounds like a lover's heartbeat.

(how your hands are another thing entirely.)

admittedly, we have made it through
without feeling the true claws of society.
because we are nothing if not sheltered
from the brunt of it; this is New York, after all.
diversity, melting pot.

but the world? they see only *big picture.*

they see your skin and my skin and think
of nothing but the differences between us.

sometimes, i think the morning will come
and it will be safe to hold you.

and it will be safe to love you in the open.
and it will be safe to love you ~~in the open~~.
and it will be safe to love ~~you in the open~~.

gentleness

there is nothing
gentleness
cannot mend.

a picket fence.

the night as it tiptoes.

a fresh dream.

something new
as it forms
in the belly
of a
giddy, giddy world.

the heart.

this is the journey

just the same

often, love looks like
growing shadows on paper walls;
full of thinly veiled desire.

it is impatient.

like piano hands,
quick and nimble,
it starts to wander.

mostly, someone is whispering,
come. come back. stay. no, stay. please.
come closer. come back. stay.

but (the door opens and closes.)
but (the handle turns.)

but (the lock clicks.)

earthquake

i have stood in my own way today
more times than anyone has closed the door.

i have yelled at myself in every language.
i have grown accustomed
to my own angry tongue.

i have spent
the better half of a lifetime
inside of a body
that does not understand
how to build something
from the ground up.

only that the ground
feels like the bottom.
only that the ground
looks like failure.

only that the ground is earthquake
and we are knobby-kneed and,

after all this time,
uncertain of our footing.

this is the journey

in a different life
---

many different women have lived in me.
adventurer, nurturer, artist.

nothing haunts me
like the lives i could have led,

if one of them had raised their hand
and not apologized for speaking.

dreaming about the wind

in the early hours,
before the rest of the world
has been set in motion,

i want to wake up
and drink from the river.

press my lips against
someone else's lips.

dream about the wind and then
be the wind.

and when no one is there
to see me,
it will be like how
in full view of the sun,
the naked eye is blind.

ten years

if i rewind ten years, i am still staring at the face of
a girl who does not understand her features yet.
she is carving out her own eyes in the mirror. she
is cursing her nose and her chin and her kinky,
unkempt, untamable hair. she is swearing at her
stretching reflection.

she is trying to erase all of the places her body has
proclaimed adulthood. she is frustrated that her
body has declared it so loudly.

she is still a child. she is still just a child. learning
that other people have opinions about her body,
and the way she carries it, and the things she does
with it. learning that she somehow both likes and
dislikes the way other people see her. she is learning
to become what she feels is desirable. she is learning
to despise the things about herself that make that
notion difficult.

she compares and imitates. wonders if it is a sin to
speak up. wonders why so many of her female peers
do not raise their hands in class, remain hushed, sit
in clusters in the corner of the schoolyard instead of
playing dodgeball. still, she bites back most of the
things she wants to say.

like, *how many raindrops can fall in an hour?* and, *is
love always forever?* and, *should i wear lip gloss for
my first kiss or do you think chapstick will be fine?*

she realizes quickly that she is not good at quiet. she
is not especially great in gym class either, but her
curiosity can run two miles in nine minutes without
blinking.

at this age, strangers ask about her ethnicity with
the same frequency they ask gas station workers for
directions. she does not know yet that she is never
required to answer.

they ask because her skin is a marching band of
colors. in the summer, a trumpet in the back row. in
the winter, a twirling baton.

she doesn't understand poetry yet. hasn't learned the
value of a journal filled with metaphors and wishes.

she is laughing at jokes she knows are not funny.

she is struggling to find the balance between what
she has and what she wishes she had.

if i rewind ten years, i am still staring at the blank
space between the knowledge of myself and the
reality of my being.

last thursday i read an article that stated, *children
struggle to understand their identity when they do not
understand their identity,* and strangely, it made sense
to me.

this is the journey

tomorrow

it is utterly terrifying
to wake up wanting
to hold your hand.

(but i'll do it again tomorrow.)

alison malee

<u>escaping</u>

enough now.

hear me when i say,
heat escapes open mouths
even when you trust them.

the sun and the dawn
both exhale steadily.

and lips find
other lips
find other lips
find other
lips.

this is the journey

that city kind

read: the biology of undoing your organs.

cottonmouth. closed fist mouth.

open. become wound. open. become wound.

if i ask nicely, will you turn me into something
    malleable? less volatile?

once, a heart. now, a gatekeeper.

i dreamt about love, and then it arrived.
took that red-eye flight from its hometown.

the evening watched as it undressed me in the back
    of a taxi.
our driver averting his eyes.

love didn't wait for front door pauses.
moved in swiftly like an alley cat. a drum solo.
something sweet and hot and rising.

if you can read this, you haven't missed a thing.

love swallowed me whole and spit me out
onto the pavement.

open. become wound. now, a gatekeeper.

the world / everything

in other words,
i am hungry.

in other words,
my desire
spills from me
in hollowing waves.

in other words,

i want, i want, i want.

this is the journey

a little room

in union square, between the trimmed back garden
and the cobblestones, a man strums an old ukulele.
the wood has faded, dipping inward
in all of the places his hands must rest
when the quiet urges him to play.

as he caresses the drooping strings,
all of the notes tightrope wobble into each other.

the subway doors peel open at 14th street,
and when i climb to the top of the stairs i see him,
his face tipped to the side as he sings
into a duct-taped makeshift microphone.

the rest of New York keeps moving.
heads down or phones on,
lit up by the immediacy of glowing screens.
a mass blur of very busy, of scarves and puffy
    jackets.

each with their own craning swan necks
bent in the usual position.

his voice wobbles as he hums and sputters,
stops, slows his way through a crawl of a song.
it is slick like eels between our ears.
graceful, too, a tambourine shimmying,
and what is the analogy for never knowing
you wanted something until it presents itself to you?

as a child, i bet he dreamt of flying.
soaring over Manhattan, flush against the clouds,
his music a parachute he strapped himself into.

this stranger standing on the corner of 16th,
making a little room for life in the pushing throng.
this stranger barely blinking at the people brushing
   past,
bumping padded shoulders.

a group of teenage girls dodge
outstretched taxi hands, giggling wildly
at some unknown joke that exists between them,
as tourists haggle over the prices at
a pretzel cart.

and me?

i pass him two worn one dollar bills
from the folds of my jeans,
but i do not stop, either.

this is the journey

you promise to love me even when i am nothing
but old skin.
it sounds like a death sentence.

alison malee

melody

my hand rests on your hand
and isn't that its own

sweet, whistled song?

this is the journey

it does not

i practice the art of It Does Not Bother Me
and on my way home from work, start a charity for
   the Bothered.

rub my smug face with my smug hands and think of
   all the things
that could bring me to tears but won't.

see, there is a roof over my head
and who cares about the inner turmoil?

not me.

see how i do not lift a finger? see how perfectly i am
   not bothered?

see how the lonely does not weep against the glass
   like a humid summer?

i park my car in the driveway, donate $5 to this sad
   cause.
open the front door.

smile a slow stretch of a smile and barely feel
   anything at all
when my eyes twitch. when my throat closes.
when my lungs hang between my knees.

when the door knob suddenly feels like a
   rattlesnake writhing against my palm.

i am so well practiced, i almost miss the heat as
my teeth open my bottom lip.

besides, no one notices anyway.

no one has ever questioned
the silence.

see? see how it does not bother me?
see how it does not bother me at all?

this is the journey

survival

the walls grow higher and higher,
and the only way to scale them is to
scale them slowly.
but the stone turns into dust over time.

it is jagged clay we have
pieced together with the heat
from our own hands.

no one understands survival
like mountain climbers
understand the drop
from the edge of a cliff.

hanging on is a necessity, not a choice.
or it is a choice that it is always a necessity.

what can anyone know about

letting go other than
sometimes it results in blood?

kindness

be kind, says mama, but i tell you
my sharp tongue is a warm companion.

be kind, says mama, but i find
this space where my mouth should be
to be an open fly trap.

be kind, says mama, but
we are all animals.

be kind, says mama, but there is
a trail of blood that follows me.

be kind, says mama, and the words
hum like flightless birds. she brushes my hair behind
  my ear.
the sugar in her voice is a familiar chorus.

be kind, says mama. so i tell her

i will try.

this is the journey

fragile

remember my rib cage? yesterday,
it was buried beneath eggshells,
the sum of which did get trampled on,

and today, it is sweating
like nervous, trembling fingers.

all my water weight
vanishes through each and every bone,

like the space between them
is a factory of mirrors
and expensive glassware.

(cracking and cracking)

tomorrow i will still be
a prisoner of my own heartbeat.

partially awake,
partially a poem slumbering.

fragile and human. human and fragile.
human and human and human.

in need of a different view

i want to look out the window
of a love that
makes me want to

let all the light fall through.

this is the journey

biological family and the return of questions

i did not know grief
could feel like second nature
until grief
was second nature.

(&) i did not know
family could feel foreign
until blood was quicksand.

(&) i did not know i could
bury hurt until ghosts
rose from soil.

(&) i did not understand empathy
until all of this hollow.

(&) i did not meet fear
until

i was terribly afraid

i was not capable
of forgiveness.

a humming in the shadows

you won't find an answer here,
but you will search for it.
it will smell like eucalyptus.
look like a lake beneath thin ice.
it will be a nightly ritual,
you wanting these things
that can't be kept.

this is that sinister magic.

a brutal fist. a handprint.
a humming in the shadows.
a tripped alarm.

everything is black. and this is not brown beautiful.
brown black beautiful.
deep black beautiful.

no, this is midnight. embers gone flat.
the underside of the moon after a long shift.

somewhere, a candle flickers and
greed spills from the flame.
i told a story once and everyone
in it was named after an old lover.
this is what it means to know lust
like the inside of the wrist;
blood blooming and blooming.

this is the journey

crooked

there is a space
between
your words.

where your smile curves.

slightly. crooked.

i can still feel that.

years later.

someone asks me if i know where my curls came from

i say, what do you call addiction if not disease? in an
ice age, a sickness like a snowstorm. a constant.

i say, of course i have always recognized my mother.
in the wrinkles of a graying cashier. in the keen
eyes of a growling bulldog. in the swaying girls in a
nightclub bathroom. in a wind chime's hollow echo.

i recognize her in the way i put myself to sleep. she
is the dried salt on wet cheeks. she is insomnia.
invasive species. land mine. she is the weight when
someone asks about family. if i know what it means
to have one.

i say, rationally i understand that drugs cannot be a
mother. a child cannot be a mother.

an addict cannot make themselves less of an addict
in a breath; in nine months. but she can decide to
have a baby. decide to give her life. decide to let her
story start somewhere.

i say, if you live in an empty house long enough, it
doesn't feel empty.

i say, eventually you fill the rooms. decorate the
walls.
meet the neighbors. get a library card. fall in love
with someone or something or all of it.

i say, my curls are the stuff of angels. a gift.
i say, *i'm alive* and doesn't that mean i have been
given so many?

this is the journey

new beginnings

it is fearful, but we crave new beginnings.

know i want to read in the silence of a library
that belongs to only our collective hands.

you will prop your feet up on my two legs,
and we will drift through worlds
while never moving anything but pages.

do you hear that in the distance? the echoing siren?
the sailor's call? the warning?

i barely do anymore. (you are my world.)

i move nothing if i have not moved you.
it is true, i am consumed by love.

but the language of this place has always been a
    little unhinged.

do you hear that in the distance?
is it not a downpour? radio static? tree roots
    unwinding?

is it not the kind of rain that washes away?

maybe the light has come to apologize for
leaving, but all the anecdotes become leeches on its
    tongue.

it even looks a little new. a little like starting over.

you will not even bat an eye.
your fingers will trace the line on the page in front
    of you.

and if it is not me you are running to,
let the running be the quickest route to freedom.
and if your legs decide to carry you to me,
let our love never feel like quicksand.

(you are my world.)

this is the journey

anxiety

does anxiety not ache
to be picked up and coddled?
is it not an envious parasite?

hunched below ground,
a cruel and unhinged inhabitant

that growls
but does not come out of hiding
unless unannounced.

and when it comes

i wither like sickness,
like a medicine-
resistant virus.

what does an invisible
darkness look like,
anyway?

i tell you, it can look like
anything.

somewhere
in the
middle

this is the journey

we met somewhere in the middle,

and the world took on the shape
of something constantly shifting.

we are rising like fog in a storm.
like an exhale on a frosted window.
like a hint of lavender
making its way out of the damp earth.

like something unimaginable
being pulled from the surface,
we are claiming our space.

it has arrived, right here,
on the sleeve of yesterday.

right here,
in the middle of a whispered
prayer.

it never will

january is here. / arrived on
the heavy-lidded eyes

of rainy evenings.

we want for nothing / desire for
everything. / take
great pleasure in / this

feeling of / being alive

for another season.

the cold has / yet to break us.

this is the journey

our fingers chase the light into a new dawn
and never, not once, catch it.

manhattan

if this isn't a coming-of-age story
i don't know what is / what are
bruised knuckles anyway? / do you live
on street corners or not? / 125th and take
the A from there / sticky hot seats
and that one broken elevator / this is
the Fourth of July in Harlem / humid heat and
apartment buildings a mile high / barbecue
in the park / all eyes on us / the baby is here
and the music is loud and my lord, girl,
that isn't how we do things / but it is / and
it isn't / look, everyone / i just / i still haven't
figured it all out / what we need is a little
bit more time / next stop / don't blink
but / i crave sidewalks / high lines / the
symphony of chaos / Manhattan / don't you
miss me, too?

this is the journey

at least halfway

it never starts out ugly. it is a clean scrape.
a brush of leg against cold feet. a half-past-morning
    alarm.
a few words lost in the tension. a belly-deep hunger.

then the door slams. first, it's a mistake.
we take it back, make love at midnight.
it's graceful and poignant and fills us to the brim.
or at least halfway. or at least almost.

the next day, the art falls. once. twice.
the painting cracks. your voice shakes.
it's all mixed-up, but still we try to repair any
    damage.

at some point, the poems begin to fester.

when the wound grows and stretches
from one end to the other, and the halls
are stick-thin quiet; we don't even yell.

you pick open the scab again and again.
it is tender and swollen, taut and angry,

i clean my hands more than necessary.
until palms peel back, dry, cracked.
carrying soap like a life raft in my back pocket.

and we say nothing, but it says everything
when we turn tail and let each other go.

<u>now, not</u>

and in one moment
we went from lovers
to strangers.

a cruel fate for us.

a parting like
the Red Sea,

split open.

a whole thing
now, not.

this is the journey

before you

before the end, it is tuesday.
we sit behind lemon trees,
hidden in our own thoughts.

the sun dips below the tops of the trees.

before the fall, it is too late to go home.
i make sure to note the way
you lick your lips.

before the blush,
i know your middle name.
we hold damp hands.

i confess i am hungry for the world.

there is tender in your eyes.

before you,
my life swings and dips.
i lazily taste youth from the spring.

let it drip down my chin.
let it sharpen my teeth.

<u>have we?</u>

shouldn't we just check /
to see if / in the quiet of our distance

we have somehow / outgrown / each other?

this is the journey

<u>(i'm not)</u>

i can be sorry for the hurt.
i can be sorry for the hurt.
i can be sorry for the hurt.

but still dig my nails in.

what we carry in our pockets

somewhere we are wading into tide pools,
catching fish with our bare hands, our stomachs full.
the sun is high, our skin is heated by the vision of
   it all.
love breathes easy.

this is the life we see dressed up in daydreams.

but we have learned to find solace in carrying lonely
like a receipt in our back pockets.

it reads: toothpaste, paper towels,
almond milk we won't drink,
frozen meals that will stay in the freezer,
pasta we will run out of by friday.

it reads bus passes—2, movie tickets—2.
all the things we do together but alone.

somewhere we are wading into tide pools.
the water is mild,
covering us both in salt and mischief.
love breathes easy, here.
we are together.

this is the journey

i tuck away the grief, but you must understand—
it still lives, it still consumes.

the officer and the iron bars

it is not too late to lick the off-white from the sky,
pretend the unrest tastes just like vanilla ice cream.

like that hot yoga class you took to prove you could.

like the betrayal you ignored to make room for
    someone
whose name ate up all of the pages of your
    notebook.

it's the year the shadows danced through an
    overgrown landscape.
no roots took hold, and the branches lapped
at the roads like demon hounds.

when the police asked how much you'd been
    drinking
and all you could see was the disappointment in
    their eyes,
i didn't blame you. it had been a long night.

you held the breathalyzer
like a bird
clutched to your chest,
willing it to grow wings
and sail from your fingers.

when i say i hope age settles you,
i mean there is more than being alive
enough.

there is more than this.

watch; ten years can change everything.

this is the journey

<u>am i lying?</u>

what if i laid my hair
across your chest?

made you count the strands,
held your breath in my own lungs,
and still left without explanation?

would you chase me
or would you understand that,
even when my mouth is closed,

i am lying?

what happens when you meet your father at twenty-four

the day you are to meet your father, you find
yourself waiting for the alarm to ring. your frazzled
eyes have been glued to the screen for hours,
propped open with a slow, cruel kind of panic.

when you get out of bed, your face twists up as
you remove your sticky legs from the sheets and
slip into the shower. you turn the water on as hot
as it will go. let the heat seep into your skin. beg
yourself to relax. relax. relax. try to make it stick
with repetition. turn the water off and dry your tree
branch limbs. put on your clothes.

it is almost inaudible over the crashing sound
of your heartbeat, but there is music playing. a
slow beat, a ballad maybe. a song your husband
is listening to in the next room. a steady rhythm.
somehow your lungs maintain a steady rhythm, too.

you whisper goodbye to your children when you go.

in the garage, you put the key in the ignition. watch
your hands as they shake violently. watch the sky
crack into a million pieces. watch rain wipe the
windshield clean.

the trip takes two hours. one hundred and twenty
minutes. seven thousand two hundred seconds
of your universe ringing in your ears. all you can
think about, on a loop, is the desperate way you
are longing for him to like you. to be proud of the
person you have become without him. to be proud
of the person you grew into all on your own.

the bus terminal's parking lot is crowded. too many
cars, too many gravelly engines huddled together in
such a tight space. you laugh nervously. clear your
throat. empty your pockets. take off your glasses
and check your phone and do anything to avoid
getting out. for a moment, you consider starting
the car again. you think about what would happen
if you merely went home. if you did not follow
through.

but instead, you pray. eyes tight and hands folded.
you don't always. don't always know if anyone is
listening. don't always understand why prayer needs
to be such a formal thing. but you ask whoever is
out there for some courage. just enough to get out of
the car. just enough for the day. and so it is nothing
short of a miracle when, eventually, your feet go
from gas pedal to pavement.

the more you think about him, the more your chest
aches. how much can one person romanticize a
scenario that has no business being folded into
pretty packaging?

a man in the distance is walking toward you, but you
do not know if it is him until you lock eyes. and oh,
the way your breath catches in your throat.

his height surprises you. you note the way his
shoulders sit up by his neck. how often you have
thought of him as a mountain in a state you have
never driven through. a familiar avalanche you must
have loved in a different life. and now, to see the man
in front of you and understand him to be family.

after all of this time, to meet a stranger who is your
father. a father who is, at best, still a stranger. a man
who is wearing your face.

breath by breath, all of the air in your lungs
vanishes. there is darkness and then there is your
lightning bolt veins. slithering electric chairs.

this is the reality of your life suddenly blinking out
and starting over.

he hugs you and his shirt smells like rain, too. like
the sky cracking into a million pieces.

you wonder if, after everything, there just may be
a god.

what happens when you meet your father at twenty-
four: you wish you could have had more time. you
hope you still do.

this is the journey

as if i am my own set of feathered wings,
i expand, terrible and haunting.

loss

why do we not talk about
the aftermath?

the pause before
i'm sorry for your loss
that hangs overhead.

swallows whole cities,
whole countries,
to fit you
in the belly of this
new, empty
space.

this is the journey

woman:

how i became a woman is not the sort of thing you
    discuss
in polite conversation, or over a pot of tea, or
    around a table
where we don't use first names and lips are pressed
    together
like lemonade can be made out of bitter expressions.

no, the tale of how i become a woman is a bar brawl,
hungover until 4 PM, teeth scraping against the
    inside of mouths,
the inside of thighs that belong to uninterested
    strangers,

the *i can't shake the feeling that i'm alone here* kind
    of story.

in another life, i may have been born flower.
velvet petals, supple, gentle. perched on a
    windowsill,
a pretty little thing to admire from afar.
but i was born warrior. all sharp, serrated edges and
    no handle.

born girl. born lanky legged and opinionated,
with words tied to my chest and no apologies among
    them.

the world is hard for women who push back.

when i say hard, i mean each wall rises up like a rock
    and a hard place.
i mean violence is a hard place.
i mean growing accustomed to harassment on the
    street is a rock.

i mean one in four, one in four, one in four is a rock.
i mean tucking keys between fingers and pocket
    knives
in our boots at night is a rock.
i mean *being a woman is a hard place.*

the ceiling is not glass. it is bulletproof.
that is why each morning i load my gun, *bullet.*
equality. *bullet.* equality. *bullet.*

learning to love myself in a world that
does not accept or acknowledge my right to love
    myself. *bullet.*

how i became a woman. *i aimed. i fired.*

this is the journey

<u>dancing</u>

what if i told you i burn houses;
i set fire to all things good.
i stay up to watch the sun rise but
feel weighed down with insignificance
every time i do.

what if i told you
i do it all for love.
i reek of battles.
i stink of gasoline.
i see flames
dancing on the wind,
and
i want you to hold my hand.

alison malee

teaching my heart to be a butcher knife
in a world of unmovable mountains and soft flesh.

this is the journey

i will remember

i will remember you in the way flames meet paper.
quickly, like if we touch too long we might become
    too tangled,
we might become too many limbs cascading
around each other; we might never leave.
that is all there is. the remembering.
now that you've read the last page of the book.
now that you have decided what *is to be* the last page.
now that you have decided that the book *needed* a
    last page.
this is only the epilogue.

how will we explain to our families around stiff-
    backed tables
that we are no longer in the same skyline?
that our hearts could not let go of our greed and
    desire
long enough to become anything but stubborn?
we were doomed from the start, they will say.
you both had such big eyes and such lust for the
    world.
we will nod, we will sit with our hands folded in our
    individual laps.
we will both say words like yes, and of course,
and we will grow comfortable in the silence.
i will miss your hand on my knee.
you will still call but only to listen to my voicemail,
never to say anything of substance.
and we will go on.

i think maybe that is the worst of it.
that we will one day
become such utter strangers that
if we were to ever be in the same place,
we wouldn't recognize each other's faces.
your voice would not make my mouth water the way
   it used to.
i would not look at your hands and see safety nets.
only hands.

this is the epilogue. the after-the-ending-has-been-
   written
pages that describe what has yet to come.
the beginning of something new.
the world as it looks without each other in it.
the space we will need to fill.
only hands.

this is the journey

nothing owns humanity like time.

anything more than

i am a shipwreck.

i am a wreck. i am a ship.

i have jumped.
with both feet.

i have been thrown
overboard.

i have been
    flagged
down.

i have called
the depth
   of the water

my home
when it wasn't

anything more
than darkness.

much love

it is nearly September when johnny writes me that
first letter, folded into a crisp, clean, prison-supplied
envelope. it shows up in my mailbox unannounced
and expected, a stray that slips in and out of
neighborhoods until it finds somewhere that fits.

hi, ali.

on a map, this is our starting point. point A. it
pirouettes between us like a heartbeat, an under the
floorboards thumping. how could i read it without
thinking of my childhood, the pulsing that lives
within me, the thread that ties me to the intricacy
of family.

it is a curse that i am so unprepared for something
as seemingly small and momentous as this. this, a
butterfly on a hillside; a tipping point.

the words are puffed chest and boastful.

you should've seen me, he says, his penmanship the
worn edge of fraying denim. *i could really play.
football, basketball, you name it.*

i imagine a peacock fluffing its feathers, his head
pecking and pecking at the wind.

our grandmother would love you.

grandmother, wrinkled and shining. i imagine her
as a sharp-eyed eagle, wrapping her feathered wings
around the weight of an entire family.

i'm writing a book. it is sort of like yours but different.
he writes this with his human hands, and his human
heart. so i imagine him as he must look to the rest of
the world, an adult, a man, an inmate, spread out on
a concrete floor in a place i have never been. his legs
crossed at the ankle, notebook paper just like this
strewn around him in waves.

we're family.

once, my best friend got bitten by a stray cat we
found behind my house. we were beside ourselves
with laughter, until her parents told her it was not,
in fact, humorous and dragged her to the doctor's
office for a rabies shot. we were so small, all we
could do was tease her. a cat had bitten her, sunk its
teeth into her naive wrist, as she nervously passed
it a bowl of whole milk. what an angry, ungrateful
beast, we thought, our shoulders bouncing. what
bad timing.

isn't it tragic, i want to whisper, that when i think of
us, i think of that defenseless cat, his lips pushed up
and snarling. isn't it sad, that this is what we share:
two parents, and an ability to defend.

isn't it wild, i want to yell, that in some ways i have
always been a stray. always been the one biting the
hand. isn't it crazy that you always have been, too.

johnny promises he won't make the same mistakes
again. he has always had the worst timing, he says,
always been in the wrong place.

i want to make him swear an oath, cross his heart,
cut his palm, spill the vow over anyone he has loved.
but johnny, i want to say. haven't you ever wondered
what part of our DNA makes us so reckless?

but instead i do not say any of those things. instead,
when i start my letter, i start with only *dear brother,*
and the pen blisters into the page. i do not tell him
about the cat, because i do not know if he would
understand. i do not tell him about the eagle, the
peacock, or that i have always imagined myself to be
a raven, dark and cawing.

instead, i write to him only about the tangible
things in my life and the ways in which i have and
have not successfully managed to avoid fate.

if for no other reason than to prove that i have, in
fact, existed all of these years, a stray taken out of
the cold heart of the city, four hours and a world
away.

motherhood

when i think about my daughters,
i think of the middle school boys
that teased me at the pool party
for wearing a shirt over my one-piece.

the white cloth smothering
the flashing beacon of my lower abdomen.
the soft chuckle i became, the trembling lowercase of
    my voice.

then, the red snow cone in all of its sugary glory,
as it leaped from the paper cup of a bull-faced boy,
his eyes the same raging color as the cherry syrup.

the cold that hit first the exposed skin of my neck,
and then the poor, unassuming shirt. the sacred coat
    of arms.

the towel that became my salvation when the
boy's mom was lured outside by the howling laughter,
and took my only lifeline inside to the washing machine.

that day, i did not, not even once,
get close enough to the water to swim.

when i think about my daughters,
i think they would not have said a word to any of them.
they would not have yelled or cowered.

my daughters would have
smiled widely and waggled their
sticky fingers.

my daughters would have
positioned both feet
squarely on the very edge of the diving board,
and unabashedly jumped right in.

this is the journey

can anything honest be done in such a way
that it deserves dismissal?

not moved,

but

moving

this is the journey

the current is a song that floods our veins.
and like the tide, *we are not moved, but moving.*

meaning the wind pushes us. meaning the trees
bend to listen to our language.

the sun presses on our backs as earnestly
as we press onward, glittering and vibrant.

we are in the fire and the fire is living;
the flames are an exhale.

we drink down the heat,
and keep putting one foot
in front of the next.

mostly, we do not seek stillness.

like the waves, we make our homes
along any shore we touch.

alison malee

it has to start somewhere, this setting yourself free.

this is the journey

spinning on

the steering wheel does not listen.

my palms are half a mile away, and my
fingers tap tap tap the beat of three cups of
coffee. spinning on without waiting
for green to appear.

i worry i will see red lights
cutting through the night and keep driving.

i can't maintain that i have not before;
         that i will not in the future.

everything everything

the heartstrings
of the moon.

a crochet set.

two small apples
nestled in a
wooden bowl
on the counter.

something
someone
told me i needed.

the worn leather binding
on an antique book.

a stray feather.

curiosity hurts my teeth.
i bite into everything.

this is the journey

my first novel

everything about my twenties is a work of fiction.

it isn't so much a bar crawl, and yet it isn't
quite a suburban brunch date either.

it isn't peanut butter spread on
that fresh bread from that one bakery or
the baby first learning to walk or
the check that needs cashed or
the neighborhood children
running through our backyard or
the hush of a room filled with
people who could become friends,
could remain strangers.

it is everything muddled together.
mint, lime, syrup.

the worn roads of a neighborhood.
the quicksand of a first love.
every train station from my first apartment
to the place i set down my suitcase
and decided not to pick it up again.
the unlearning. the unlearning.

(the protagonist remembers everything except
the things she can't remember
from this decade.

the plot develops over a period of time,

in which the protagonist
falls in love repeatedly with everything the world has
    to offer

but herself.

on a wednesday of the fifth year
she sits at a bar and waits for a table.
orders a drink in which none of the ingredients are
    familiar.

a man walks in and folds himself into the seat beside
    her.
she curls up her lips but does not speak to him,

and in this small moment
wonders how the protagonist in a novel she is
mainly writing on napkins would feel about her
    evening.

she thinks that woman would be proud.)

this is the journey

all this love rolling off my tongue.

alison malee

a new thing

spring
  April, May, June

arrives and takes
no prisoners.

a rippling mirage
made solid.

i know you
  as a new

thing.

this is the journey

thankful

the baby is
crying in the kitchen.

the baby is
always in need
of something.

hush now, child,
pat tears dry,
kiss, kiss again,
sway, rock, bounce
mama is here.

the toddler is asking
for a snack,
a movie,
a snack, a movie,
mama are you listening
mama can you hear me

a movie
please turn on
a movie

can i have a snack
pretty please
mama
can you hear me

hush now, child,
have you been a good listener,
yes child, a good listener,
a snack after dinner.
let's eat dinner, child.

dinner
is burning.

dinner is
sautéing onions
over low heat,
garlic, oil,
watch wait.

brown and
add to the chili pot.
simmer. simmer.

not too much spice.

come,
sit at the table,
say your prayers,
say grace,
ask for what
you need not
what you want.

say you are thankful, child.
yes, thankful,
there is food on the table
people who love you
a sun that sits on
the horizon,
a sun
that is and will be, child,
just like you.

this is the journey

hands

it is not really about anger
or disposition
because
even when i am a rose
there are still thorns.

it is more
a question of
whether my thorns and i
draw blood solely because
we have claws
or because we are touched
by wild, untrained hands.

golden years

age will teach you ten different smiles,
and all of them will mean
the same thing if you look closely.

all of mine have whispered

i want to be someone who knows
they are worth celebrating.

this is the journey

at least learn to grow something from this.

the city that never sleeps

all of the versions of me
that are still
young
hot heavy
and thriving
enough to dream

about being someone
different than the someone
i am now,

miss New York
like an
incarcerated limb,
or a house cat

accidentally

left outside
in another
unforgiving
Manhattan
winter.

tireless man

this year is all gratitude.
for you, the dust that you rose from,
not the phantom who could have been
but a thunder wielder, wild-eyed bringer of life.
for you, on Sundays, when the smell of breakfast
squeezes itself under the doorframe.
for you, always like this, always a simple sway
of breath and cheeks and knowing.
for you, as i call you forever, as i call you a home,
as i call you a lighter body.
for you, at the end of the day, when we both
nestle into the comfort of each other's weary bones.
for you, the sleep smudged around your mouth,
the slow arm you lift to drape around my chest.
for you, your calloused fingers kneading
small circles over the soft dough of my stomach.
for you, upturned sun. for you, off-key singer.
sounding board with controls yanked upward,
wind chime clank of laughter.
for you, the quiet, curious voice that stumbles
as you ask me why i like to make love to you.
for you, and the most truthful answer i can give;
there is some intimacy that does not call for
    language.
that does not need a poem or a song or a wall in
    a gallery.
this year is all gratitude.
for you, brave sailor. glass-bottom boat.
clear blue water. windswept sail. sky warrior.
    husband.

something holy

another year rings
like a bright yellow chord, and

each month the blood blossoms,
pooling like hot oil.

runs like a river between your hips,
and they say,
there are many
different kinds of worship,

but you've only ever
witnessed this one.

this is the journey

there is still a story in my lungs.

the reason we moved to the suburbs

the space to run. the space is a mercy.

i call to you and your answer
is the crackling of firewood.
in the living room,
we sing a whispered prayer.
on the porch,
we stretch solely because we can.

we are both marveling at
the way the world somehow sits closer to heaven
    here.

i take the sky into my withered arms.

my breath, salt water. the sky, honey.

isn't that why we are here,
to sew our own memories into moments not
made by the hands of men.

to be our own thread. to be our own needle.

this is my quilt. it is made of smoke.
of laughter, of wind. of running and playing
and rambunctious joy. it is made of stars.

there is space. and isn't that why we stay?

this is the journey

moment

the quiet, unsuspecting
intimacy of now,
this very moment.

what a victory
it is to be alive
and still believe
in something.

fade away

this is such a remarkably
human thing we do,
wanting even heartache to
sound like bass guitars.
fireside war stories.
busy bees swarming.

do we know how
to want anything
that is good for us?

how perpetually
we think love
should feel
as irate as
the prick of a needle.

it is well after all the notes
fade away
that we question
why we cling to what does
not cling, in turn, to us.

this is the journey

continuously

it is okay to admit that
your wounds are still open.
that you are still healing.

it takes time. *it takes time.*

danger

what monstrous anxiety
my body houses.
a quiet violence. a homing signal.

poised like a waiting drum,
my chest bears this warning label:

danger. danger.

what god decided on
my punishment?

this quick, trapped bird.
wild-winged animal.

beating. beating.

what do i desire?

let me be the impossible.
let me furnish this space
with beautiful things,

things
that do not look so much like
the sinking gravity of
black holes.

let me say,
*i am terribly confined
to the shelter of my skin,*

and let it be a
falsehood.

this is the journey

those words

here.

//

the only place
that matters.

//

do you believe in miracles?

//

my father once told me
i was beautiful.

//

i carry those words.
i carry them with me.

//

everywhere.

i hear wings outside my window
and it sounds something like hope.

don't you think?

this is the journey

<u>say</u>

say the day began sweetly.

say the day was
beginning
and so it was sweet.

say the sweetness
began as the day
opened.

say the day opened,
and everything in it
tasted like glaze
dripping from
the side of something fresh.

say everything
was fresh,
and everything held
something sweet,
and every day
was its own beginning.

say we are
our own beginning, too.

a tangible thing

long after this love
became a poem

and not a tangible thing anymore,

i am still braiding
your voice into my hair.

the primal nature

there is nothing to be found in the bedroom, they
    tell me.
full moon leaves a whispered hue across the sheets.

some nights there will be a wolf,
all claws and yellow eyes, sleeping next to you.

and you will feel the blood drawn slowly, almost as
    if by mistake.
the moon will change. a ripe grapefruit and then a
    light switch dimming.

you will ask for fresh air and still be found wanting.
maybe it will be too gentle, the paws of a great beast
tamed by insufficient time apart,
or too little passion reflecting in your eyes.

maybe you will be more sky than lover,
a little too night.
it will call you a thief, they say,
insist you steal stars from the window.

but i have always known the ways of this.
of nightgowns raised and hands searching.
it does not frighten me like it's supposed to.
i have always wondered about teeth,
if they have to injure to draw attention.

if new skin has to close over before dawn or if,
by some slight miracle, the animal hides the man
    only out of necessity.

femininity

it took me years to learn
that grace came from spine
and not from dainty hands.

feverish

i arise from the underbrush of dreams,
wingless and stranded.

every name i have ever known
sounds like concrete
being poured into both ears.

i recognize nothing
but the pulsing insistence
that i must get back
to dreaming.

these burning windows
in my bedroom must be
metaphors for something.
yes, i see flames because i am
overheating in the hands of normalcy.

feverish with need.

alison malee

what must you do in this life but be courageous?
grace filled and riotous. a lovely, frightening wonder.

this is the journey

dear forgiveness,

today i came searching for you.
beneath my eyelids, where i thought the problem
    lived.
beneath skin, where i've fought half of my battles
    and only won a few.
between lips, where angry words have spilled out
unintentionally time and time again.
you were not there.

i found, instead, a version of myself turned over
    by guilt.
guilt that sat on my chest angrily, hungrily,
picking apart my bones like a hunter's fresh kill.

yet there was no salt to preserve the mess of me.

between bones swam
only misplaced hymns,
half-uttered apologies,
and a string of jewelry my mother
passed down
that i hold onto for safekeeping.

dear forgiveness,
perhaps we need to meet on common ground.
it seems, over the years, we have become estranged.
i will admit, i have been short-tempered and
have not always greeted you with open arms,
if i have greeted you at all.
i am sorry for leaving you so long alone.

this time, though, this time i am ready.
i have cleaned out my attic and made peace with
    my enemies.

i opened up all of the windows.
aired out the drapes. turned on the fan.
watched the sun tiptoe slowly across the walls.

it has done wonders.

dear forgiveness,
if i can learn to forgive myself,
i think i am still salvageable.

this is the journey

faith needed a home and so i built one.
(i am the home.)

marriage vows worn thin and made new

my lungs fold around a promise.
it is as frail as paper dolls,
as tilting as cardboard marionettes.

a vow slips between my ears
and out from the gaps in my teeth.

it falls off of my shoulders like loose sleeves,
and word by word,

lands in a heaping pile on the floor.

after some time, i will return it
to the junk drawer in the kitchen.

or perhaps, i will air it out on a clothesline in the
    yard.
pin the corners up. pull it tightly.

as it sways in the wind, i will ask for eloquence,
and in the end, it will sound like this:

it is a glorious thing, to know
i could spend
the next fifty years loving you.

this is the journey

adoption rings another bell

with my mother's leaving /
it is not clear how i came to know you /

the old superstition / about unwanted things /

six weeks isn't enough /

to know someone / six weeks isn't enough
to want to vanish / but / thin air, they say /

are we the same / do you think we could be /

is it okay / to want to have at least / this / in common /

i keep running, too / shower left on / until
water tank sizzles /

it isn't romantic / hasn't ever been /

there is no applause waiting /
no slow and steady build / no significance /

i have never /
forgiven myself / not for anything /

not for the unknown / or unsaid

questioning /

was it / somehow / my fault

want

want is
that sick panic.

the kind that yanks
heartache
from the attic.

want
is knees pressed
    tightly.

want is holding on.
want is derailment.

want is
waiting impatiently
for the doorbell

and then

the slow, slow
    sweat
of having to
say hello.

this is the journey

the back of a living thing

the therapist leans back in his chair,
his arm swung wide around the wooden shoulders.

what you have to understand, he says,
motioning with his hands for emphasis,
is that a chocolate lab cannot become a coffee table.

he says, a coffee table is the same height
as a chocolate lab, and of course, has four sturdy legs.

he adjusts his own legs to demonstrate.

but the differences between them are so vast,
it would be impossible for one to become the other.
he pauses, and looks at me so intently
that i find myself nodding in agreement.

around the end of his pen, he asks if i understand
    this analogy.

but my ears are filled with the buzz
of the air conditioning,
the doors down the hall opening and closing,
the shush of the carpet as feet pad between rooms.

i hear the words, but they ring at the same pitch as the
little cymbals a toy monkey crashes into each other
if you turn the key on his back.

the tension in the air is a tight fist.
my throat closes and reopens as a drawbridge
    straddling a desert ravine.
i say, is it wrong that i would willingly set my coffee
    cup
on the back of a living thing
with four working limbs,
just to see if maybe, it would stay there for a while?

the therapist sighs,
and takes another sip from his water glass.

is that what you want to do?

spend your life cleaning up a mess
every time the doorbell rings,
and the dog goes off,
running after something else?

this is the journey

a night out

i sweat. i dance.

i swipe on lipstick like
a wax seal to parchment
and feel beautiful.

without prompting,
i rearrange myself into poses
for the full-length mirror,
and for once do not look away.

outside, my grin is just
as much for me
as it is
for passing strangers,

and laughter finds me
like hot breath,
mouth to mouth,
amen amen.

for the evening,
though it may be short-lived,

the world and i share
one staggering heartbeat.

flaws

my clenched stomach is its own weapon,
and my butterfly veins grow more and more
    envious of the statuesque muscle.

can addiction spit you out in the same way if you
    aren't addicted?

it is an inevitability that i will ask the same questions
    and get the same answers.

i hold an annual meeting with myself in which we
    discuss the problematic way i handle
any and all confrontation, and neither of us says
    a word.

love continues to unravel me.

i check the mail. check the mail. check the mail.
    check the mail. check the mail.

wipe my sweaty hands on my jeans.

check the mail again.

this is the journey

close your eyes and see if anything matters if you
cannot remember what it felt like.

hair

on the eve of my birthday,
i find myself gathering courage
in the same manner
i gather loose strands of hair.

i know this because none of it stays
where i put it, and i am
sweaty and frustrated in the pursuit.

by the end, i still have all of these
tiny, frizzy pieces floating
about the outskirts of my face.

i know this because
i have had three different last names
and none of them have fit quite right.

sometimes i think about shutting down,
and do; right then and there.

in any event, i wanted to tell you that, recently,
some days i wake up and
let bravery bounce around my curls.

decide to

leave my hair down.

this is the journey

buttercream

when the clock strikes,
the windows begin to fog with
that buttercream of evening.

have you ever been outside
when someone throws
themselves into that milky dusk?
head first, arms back.

wait until the sun rises,
and my feet hit that warm, warm earth.

if it wasn't for all of this human, i would howl.

i would let out a roar from
the very recesses of my throat.

i still might.

i still don't

i sit on the edge of a window seat. / contemplate
  how almost every idea i have had. /
about myself. / is wrong. /

it can change that quickly, that is what they do not
  tell you. /

one moment you are one person. the next moment
  you are staring at yourself through contaminated
  smog. /

your nose is the same odd shape, and your hair is
  the same length, and you still have that one dimple
  at the corner of your mouth. but it's all wrong.
  distorted. foreign. alien. /

i don't cry for days, and when i do, i have to will the
  tears to come. /

can numbness shatter you? depending. are you made
  of glass or concrete? /

always been a funny, addicted little thing. / glass. all
  glass. /
two shades too pale and one shade too dark. /
made of too much camouflage. /

if you think you know me, you don't. / how can
  you? /

i still don't even. / know myself. /
i still don't even. / know if i want to.

this is the journey

what i think she means

i ask my three-year-old what she would say to
someone if she wanted to compliment them. what
she would want to say to a friend, or a loved one, if
she wanted to say something really nice.

she pauses for a moment, all babbling brook giggles
and secretive smiles. at this age, she still thinks of
herself as a spy, a princess, a dinosaur. she thinks
we are a team. our backs flush against each other at
the scene of the crime, posed for our next adventure.

my daughter is a miniature teenager, constantly
questioning, constantly pushing the limits. she raises
her hand almost as much as she raises her voice, and
she does both of these things so often, planes land
in our living room out of respect.

after some thought, there is a tug on my sleeve. she
whispers, *i would say, thank you.*

i nod slowly, sure that this is her response solely
because we are in the process of teaching her
manners.
she leans her body up against my leg and i curl my
arms around her knobby shoulders as i kiss her
brow.

what would you be saying thank you for? i ask, *did i
hand you something? did i give you a present?*

her little nose scrunches into a strawberry field. she
laughs, and her eyes are a crisp horizon.

no, mommy. thanks for you.

in truth, there isn't much she doesn't know
already. her young mind consumes everything like a
swirling tidal wave. she is still absorbing. picking up
every detail.

maybe she doesn't understand the bigger, harder
points yet. the hierarchy of civilization. politics.
climate change. but she gets it. this whole living
thing.

what i think she means is, there is too much and
there is everything. i am thankful for all of it.

what i think she means is, *i love you.*

this is the journey

waiting

my heart is in my throat.
is on the floor.
is in my throat again.
is walking away from me.
is sticking out its tongue
when i yell, *come back here.*
is darting into oncoming traffic.
is tightrope walking.
is falling in love with people
who carry ghosts in their wallets.
is a ghost.
is stuck in the confines
of a hand.
is stuck in the confines
of being an organ.
of wanting so many things.
of wanting too
many people.
is always waiting for
someone to want it
with the same
ferocity.
is always
w a i t
     i n g.

it isn't

and wouldn't you love
it if i made this

anxiety / depression /
grief / anger /
human emotion

into something bite sized?
should it only fit
around a pinky finger?
disappear when asked?

be
smaller than
the top of a thimble?

unnoticeable?
microscopic?

you
would like that.

but it isn't.

this is the journey

<u>you may not be able to see it</u>

give me permission to be miserable.
let me play chess with my grief.
wallow. cry. come up for air.

make ten grocery lists. stay home. eat breakfast for
    dinner.
do not try to make light of it.

give me

time to process. computer paper notes. gentle
    reminders.
maps and tracking numbers and email updates and
    directions.

tell me you are just checking to make sure i got
    home alright,

because there is not much that makes me feel safer
than knowing you want me to be safe.

and i know it isn't tangible,
but it has, butter and jam, spread through my lungs.

you may not be able to see it, but this joy

costs.

oh, how possible it is to live.

this is the journey

all i can tell you

all i can tell you
is that the women
i know are not fiddling
with their thumbs.

are not teacup women,
little fragile women.

the women i know
are loud like lightning,
crack, boom.

loud like thunder,
loud like
overcome.

like indescribable
adversity
will not stop us,
halt us,
slow us.

loud like snap,
like applause.

like do *you* know
who *we* are.

loud like
change.

loud like
it is time to work.

loud like riot. like whisper.

like
women that
softly,
gently,

yank the closed door
off of the hinges,
and say

thank you.

loud

like just wait
until you meet us.

this is the journey

let the juice run

if i think about the ocean long enough, i grow fins.
it is midmorning as i write this, and in my mind
they slither down my limbs; squeeze like
a pair of jeans right before the seams burst.
does that make sense? all i know is this is
the only way i can explain it, and i still find myself
    asking,
do i need permission to be this restless?

why it's been a year since i last saw a rolling tide,
    i don't know.
money, i suppose. time. what do you do when you
    don't have much of either?
eat too many desserts and buy $10 t-shirts.
drink red wine on the deck and get sunburn from all
    that yard work.
listen to a child sing you a song you are pretty sure is
    not actually a song.
recite a poem you know by heart. curse when you
    stub your toe on the sidewalk.
paint a canvas from the craft store and call it art.
wish on every firefly. catch them and let them go
    immediately.
call it a good life. mostly, because it is.

the only way to live is to live.
every other rule book makes it complicated, but look;
just bite into a peach and let the juice run.
wake up in the dark to nurse the baby.
fall asleep to the sound of breathing and creaky
    floors.
roll the windows down. listen. use your manners.

be as outrageous as you like.
tell your people that you do, in fact, love them.
even when you can't swim to the surface.
even when the ocean swirls in your memory.
even when the fins claw up through your bones.

tell them. tell them, anyway. call it a good life.

this is the journey

learning to catch fireflies with honey instead of
hands. *this is the journey.*

index

index

this is the journey

Andrews McMeel Publishing
a division of Andrews McMeel Universal
1130 Walnut Street, Kansas City, Missouri 64106

www.andrewsmcmeel.com

19 20 21 22 23 BVG 10 9 8 7 6 5 4 3 2 1

ISBN: 978-1-4494-9299-1

Library of Congress Control Number: 2018965612

Handwritten type by Kathrin Seigel

Editor: Patty Rice
Designer/Art Director: Julie Barnes
Production Editor: Elizabeth A. Garcia
Production Manager: Cliff Koehler

Attention: Schools and Businesses

Andrews McMeel books are available at quantity discounts
with bulk purchase for educational, business, or sales
promotional use. For information, please e-mail the
Andrews McMeel Publishing Special Sales Department:
specialsales@amuniversal.com.